W9-CIP-594

Why Is the Grass Green?

A **Just Ask** Book

Hi, my name is
Christopher!

by Chris Arvetis
and Carole Palmer

illustrated by James Buckley

Rand McNally & Company

Chicago / New York / San Francisco

I'm looking at the grass.
Look how green it is.
Every little piece is green.

It certainly is !

I wonder why.
Can you tell me—
why is the grass
green?

Well, Christopher,
stop and look around you.
It's not just the grass
that's green.
Almost all the plants
here are green.

I never knew that!

And the plants all
have leaves.
But the leaves look
different from each other.
They come in many
shapes and sizes.

Let's find out
about leaves.

Look at that little bud,
Christopher.

It is the beginning
of a tiny leaf.

As the sun warms the bud,
the leaf starts to grow
The leaf has many parts
we can't see with our eyes.
Let's look at a drawing.
It will help you understand.

Let's pretend we can look inside the leaf.
See the special little green parts?
They contain CHLOROPHYLL.
Say CHLO-RO-PHYLL with me.

CHLO-RO-PHYLL !

The leaf needs chlorophyll.

The leaf uses the chlorophyll to help make a special food for the whole plant.

Let's see what else the leaf needs.

Mmm, tastes good!

The leaf needs sunlight.
It gets light and energy
from the sun.

The warm sun
feels good!

The leaf needs water.
The plant's roots bring
water to the leaf.

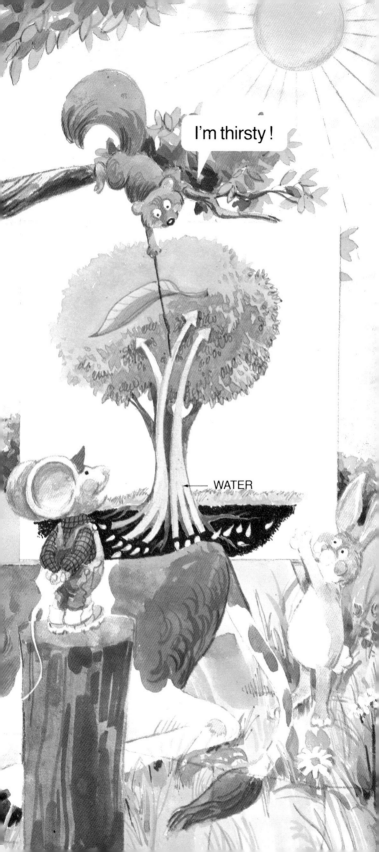

The leaf also needs
carbon dioxide.

We can't see carbon dioxide,
but it is a gas in the air.

The green chlorophyll is
very important.

It takes in the sunlight
that makes the whole
plant grow.

Let's see how…

I can't see it!

You can't see it!

Can you?

It's in the air!

Each leaf is like a tiny little factory that makes a special food for the plant.

The factory uses sunlight, water, carbon dioxide and chlorophyll.

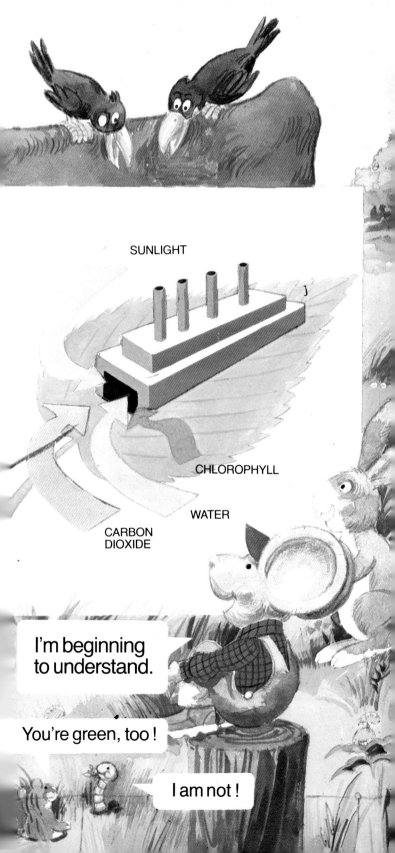

CHLOROPHYLL

CARBON
DIOXIDE

WATER

As the plant makes its food,
it gives off another gas
called oxygen.
All of us need oxygen
to live and grow.

Now we see how the little
leaf factories use the light
from the sun, carbon dioxide
from the air, water from the
roots, and the green
chlorophyll in the leaf
to make the plant's food.

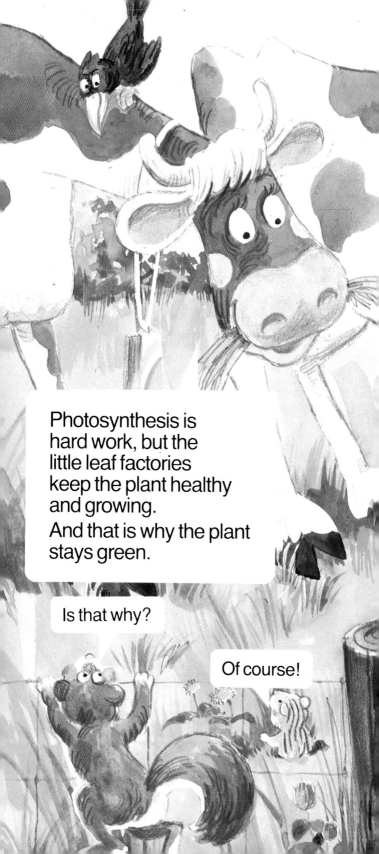